T0199169

GOD

MOVES ME . . .

nursenicholette

WestBow Press books may be ordered through booksellers or by contacting:

WestBow Press
A Division of Thomas Nelson & Zondervan
1663 Liberty Drive
Bloomington, IN 47403
www.westbowpress.com
1 (866) 928-1240

Scripture taken from the Holy Bible, NEW INTERNATIONAL VERSION®, NIV® Copyright © 1973, 1978, 1984, 2011 by Biblica, Inc.® Used by permission. All rights reserved worldwide.

This book is a work of non-fiction. Unless otherwise noted, the author and the publisher make no explicit guarantees as to the accuracy of the information contained in this book and in some cases, names of people and places have been altered to protect their privacy.

ISBN: 978-1-9736-5931-0 (sc)
ISBN: 978-1-9736-5932-7 (e)

Library of Congress Control Number: 2019904169

Print information available on the last page.

WestBow Press rev. date: 4/23/2019

WESTBOW
PRESS®
A DIVISION OF THOMAS NELSON
& ZONDERVAN

Acknowledgements

To my loving parents William Frances and Joan Ann who always taught their children to follow the 10 commandments, as they believe this is how we honor God with our life.

My Grandmother Martha is the first story in this book. Her drawing on the cover expresses what unconditional love looks like. As an artist, she had created many Christian- themed paintings, although I had never recognized this to be one of them. It was revealed to my husband many years later that this might not be my Grandfather holding one of his granddaughters' right hand. Is it possibly our Heavenly Father, "who takes hold of your right hand and says to you, Do not fear; I will help you." (Isiah 41:13).

I am truly blessed with the love, support, and encouragement that I received from my husband Howard and my favorite son Christopher while on this journey, authoring my book.

Blessed thanks to Cape Cod Karen who encouraged me to write down my stories, along with my brother-in-law Calvin who also pressed me to write this book to tell of God's ever presence in our lives and how He uses us to do His good works. Thank you also to Donna and Melva my pray warriors who encouraged me, as I believe that God faithfully placed you in my life for His purpose and plan. Many thanks to WESTBOW Press for providing support, tools and the wonderful opportunity to work with you in publishing this book. God Bless.

Planting the Seed

I still love to ride my bicycle, maybe not as fast or as far as I used to, but it is time alone with my Heavenly Father. I enjoy all He has created, listening to His earthly orchestra of nature and seeing His beauty and magnificence in everything.

"I will praise you, O Lord, with all my heart; I will tell of all your wonders." Psalm 9:1.

In the year 1975, driving illegally with my Grandmother in her mustard color Dodge Dart, I learned about Servanthood. At age 17 and her at 69, between the two of us, we only had our learner permits, albeit we laughed and concluded two learners permits were just as good as one drivers license, along with the fact that my Grandmother looked pretty good driving that car.

Together, we traveled the back roads of Pendleton, New York through the country side as we delivered her fresh- baked bread and barley soup. This not only opened my eyes- it touched my heart and soul. For the first time in my life, I saw such a cosmic spectrum of neediness; in the people less fortunate than my Grandmother with her "humble" soup and bread of "humility" that were shared. I watched her love of the Lord as she gently showed me how to become the hands and feet of Jesus, demonstrating His unconditional love for all of us.

I spent many summers at my Grandmother's house, packing up my suitcase on the last day of school, hopping on my 10 speed bike, never truly knowing then, the opportunities that God would have for me to do His work. I do remember one very hot day in July when I asked the "Lord to refresh my soul, forgive my sins, and let me learn to love Him more." Looking back, I can see now that I have a lot of growing up to do –nevertheless- I was on the path.

Martha, my Grandmother, was a woman of faith; she loved the Lord, was devoted to her family and church, a prayer warrior, an artist, a lover of life, friend to all, and an inspiration to many. "God is not unjust; He will not forget your work and the love you have shown Him as you have helped His people." Hebrews 6:10.

The Seven Year Itch

I was a Corporal at the Federal Reserve Bank (FRB) Law Enforcement Unit in Buffalo New York, transferring to FRB of Cleveland in 1984, and the following year I was married.

My son was born Labor Day weekend 1989 and within 18 months I was a single parent. This was one of the most difficult times in my life. Thank goodness for John and Val my next-door neighbors and work friends who provided love, friendship and support. These are the times; I look back, realizing God was with us every step of the way, waiting for me to return to Him.

I kept my son busy during the winter months with visits to the library for story time and toddler gym classes. When the warmer weather arrived, I rode my bicycle as he sat behind me securely in his bike seat. Receiving a bonus at work, I purchased a baby jogger, discovering my passion for running and races and my sons' enjoyment of now having a front row seat for the ride.

After a couple of years, I started dating this wonderful man to whom I am still married. Thanks be to God at age 10, Christopher asked my husband Howard to adopt him. Happily saying yes, and feeling honored, he went to our county magistrate to request the paperwork. This is when we learned that our marriage certificate was never received at the state capitol. We began to encounter many comments from friends and family about living in sin for the past 7 years, although the reality of this could have been catastrophic for all of us down the road.

We immediately returned to the Parish, recommitted our wedding vows and had Diane our maid of honor and friend re-sign that legal document as our witness. We took that legal document and drove straight to the county courthouse. On June 15th, 2000 an anniversary we still celebrate; my son was legally adopted. He changed his middle name to Howard along with taking his last name, but the best name of all that come from this story was my son calling this wonderful man-"Dad."

"Sons are a heritage from the Lord, children a reward from Him." Psalm 127:3

Love One Another

In 1998 I graduated from nursing school and was excited to begin my second career as a Registered Nurse (RN). At that time we also built and purchased a new home. There were many challenges surrounding this move with complications in regard to city services, school districts, winter maintenance on our road, and even the postal service that would deliver the mail as late as 6 or 7 o'clock in the evening or not deliver it all.

One afternoon, I drove to the post office to pick up our mail, looking for responses to the numerous resumes and applications I had sent out to area hospitals. Upon exiting my car in the Post Office parking lot, I saw a gentleman with a prosthetic leg slip and fall, I watched him struggle as his prosthesis rolled further away from him. I ran over to assist, telling him I was not sure what to do? As he guided me to proper placement and fitting, and verbalizing he felt all was secure and intact, he was ready to stand up, and just then another person came over to assist us.

Once we had gotten this gentleman standing, he turned his head and looking intently into my eyes he said "You will be an excellent nurse one day." How did he know? I had never said who I was or why I was there. Speechless I hurriedly went into the Post Office to retrieve my mail and when I reached the outside he was gone, no sign of him anywhere.

As I was driving home, a sweet aroma filled my car; I was awestruck as I knew it was him, the gentleman from the parking lot. I burst into tears...tears of joy! Appreciatively realizing "Do not forget to show hospitality to strangers, for by so doing some people have shown hospitality to angels without knowing it." Hebrews 13:2.

After that, it did not take long to begin my nursing profession taking a position on a cardiac step down unit. As my husband has always said the heart is my symbol. I have to agree there is no greater gift to give or to receive than love.

The Gardeners Tools

As my career was well on its way, the neighborhood in which we purchased our new home was governed by a Home Owners Association (HOA). Unfortunately we were not informed prior to building our cape cod, until the final day when our realtor handed us our keys and the manual regarding all the rules and regulations. My husband and I felt stifled as we casually perused through and read some of the restrictions.

The situation and location in this development continued to be problematic, many neighbors were not happy as our home and one other house, was smaller than their large "Five windows across the top" colonial cookie cutter homes. We were told by our neighbors that the previous developer promised that only certain size homes in a specific price range would be built in this development and our home depreciated their real estate and property values. Well that was the first and the last HOA meeting I attended!

So, this is where in my life, Cape Cod Karen befriended me. Looking back, the task that God had entrusted her to was not an easy one. I was still an infant in my faith hardly able to stand and had much to learn and grow by. Over time we became good friends. We went for nightly walks through our neighborhood; she continually fed me the Good Word, prayed for me and invited me to a Women's Conference where I accepted Jesus as my Lord and Savior changing my life forever!

I faithfully read my Bible daily and was slowly being transformed through the Word of God. I now understand there must be a conversion of the heart, along with the staying power of patience and the humble surrender of my stubborn self- preservation.

"Search me, O God, and know my heart; test me and know my anxious thoughts. See if there is any offensive way in me, and lead me in the way of everlasting." Psalm 139:23-24.

Working the Soul

Now a greater concern came about when our son and others became ill with severe respiratory infections believed to be caused by the older elementary schools heating system. Following some testing of the air quality and results, the school district offered to bus children to a smaller newer elementary school located in the country.

Thankfully the church we were attending embraced loved and welcomed us into their family of faith. As my heart continued to fill with love for the Lord, I became a Eucharist Minister along with taking the sacred opportunity to teach 4th grade Parish School Religion (PSR) in our home, as that was the grade my son was in. He also became an altar server and joined the children's choir.

"When your words came, I ate them; they were my joy and heart's delight, for I bear your name, O Lord God Almighty" Jeremiah 15:16

One of my greatest pleasures was to share the Word of God with whoever I could. Therefore every Monday night for PSR, using a different colored piece of chalk, I would write a Bible verse on the rock outside of our front door. Each child would study the verse, ring the doorbell, recite the verse and then enter our home. Not only did the children/students enjoy this, they were learning to memorize and recite scripture and I was sharing and proclaiming the Word of God to others!

The women who assisted with the children's choir at our church were also instrumental in sharing their love for the Lord, not only to my son, but to all the children. It just seemed that for some reason they took a special interest in my son, commenting on his sparkling deep blue eyes and dark brown hair, although more importantly they recognized his heart for Jesus.

"Let the little children come to me, and do not hinder them, for the kingdom of heaven belongs to these." Matthew 19:14.

How We Grow to Believe

Being very involved in our sons' life, one morning we drove him to the little elementary school in the country and then ventured out to enjoy a ride in the countryside. As we turned down the first street off the state route we came upon a newly built little white ranch for sale. We continued to drive and spoke about how nice it would be to live out here, then at the same time we agreed to turn around and take a look at that little white ranch. Pulling up the crackling stone driveway reminded me of the long gravel driveway that lead to my Grandmother's house in the country. We both commented on the large white pillars that adorned the front porch. There was a construction worker inside that allowed us to enter, once inside we found a large country kitchen and beautiful wooden Amish mantel surrounding a huge fireplace in the living room, and unintentionally we just found our new home.

I was off for a couple months on medical leave so I decided to put our house on the market for sale by owner. I had nothing else to do, although understanding whoever lived here would endure the same difficulties, so I prayed to my Heavenly Father for wisdom and guidance.

One evening after I had just closed my Bible our phone rang, it was a neighbor who lived in the development. They stated a relative had always liked our home and was possibly interested in purchasing it as a seasonal home to winter in. I informed them of the open house I was having the upcoming weekend and also offered that they could come anytime, understanding they lived in another state. As I hung up the phone smiling, I remember saying "Wow God, that was easy!" again feeling the closeness of my Heavenly Father and His gifts of love, mercy and compassion. The house was sold within the next couple of weeks and out to the country we moved.

"For I know the plans I have for you, declares the Lord, plans to prosper you and not to harm you, plans to give you hope and future. Then you will call upon me, and I will listen to you. You will seek me and find me when you seek me with all our heart" Jeremiah 29:11-13

God's Country

We moved into what we now refer to as our "Retirement Ranch." The blessings began when we obtained the keys to our new home on **Friday the 13th,** thankfully enough, it was also Good Friday. Cape Cod Karen came out and helped paint the big country kitchen agreeing this was the most important room in the house to set up first. We moved as much as we could on Good Friday and Holy Saturday as that Sunday was Easter Sunday, and I had to work.

Getting up early Easter Sunday morning I was extremely stiff and sore and wasn't even sure how to get to the hospital. Once at work, assessing my patients, one patient had a special request asking me if I had a crucifix. He stated he wished he was lying in his own bed and praying to the crucifix on the bedroom wall. I explained to him the hospital Volunteers had given me a bag of rosaries and was not sure if they had a crucifix or cross. I asked him to give me a few minutes to check on my other patients and then I would go to my locker.

As God would have it, the little plastic rosary did have a crucifix and not a cross. Returning to his room and looking up at me, he stated he knew he came here to die; I instantly felt ashamed and embarrassed for my complaining about how sore I was from painting and moving all weekend. Handing him the rosary with the crucifix, I leaned over and kissed him on the right cheek, smiling and telling him I was his nurse for the day.

I was off until Wednesday and during my first watch back, staff members kept telling me that the wife of the patient I took care of on Easter Sunday was looking for me as she wanted to speak to me. After some thought, I recalled the kiss on his cheek and now wondered if I possibly violated my duty as a nurse or my new profession.

Finally midway thru my shift she arrived, asking me to step into her husband's room, my heart began to race. As we entered the room, she asked if I was the nurse who gave her husband the rosary and kissed him. I said "yes." She thanked me stating that was the most compassion anyone had shown her husband in quite some time, since he has been ill. Still looking intently at me she stated "I recognize you from the church, you have that lovely boy with the sparkling deep blue eyes and dark brown hair that sang in our children's choir where I volunteered." Instantly I felt the love and compassion from my Heavenly Father with an understanding that He is directing my path.

Within a few weeks her husband was transferred to another floor. I went to visit him as often as I could and would pray with and for him. I am now beginning to believe everything that happens is orchestrated by God. He places people in our lives for a reason or a season for His purpose. I had one last opportunity to visit my patient, as he was surrounded by his wife Rose and their children; I leaned over and kissed him the second time, whispering in his ear, "say hello to Jesus for me."

"Yet I am always with you; you hold me by my right hand. You guide me with your counsel, and afterward you will take me into glory."Psalm73:23-24.

Having the Faith of a Mustard seed

The following spring 2002 my husband was diagnosed with Non-Hodgkin's Lymphoma (NHL). I cannot express the gratitude I had for the nurses and the doctors I learned to trust and appreciate at the hospital where I worked. The oncologist wanted to use a new chemo drug that became available that was demonstrating much success for patients diagnosed with NHL.

As his wife and his nurse, I was leery of my husband taking any new medication, understanding there is no literature or supporting documentation in regard to some of the side effects of this drug. I was concerned with how he would tolerate his treatments and the long-term effects over the next five to ten years. After having some of the larger lymph nodes surgically removed from his neck for palliative care, others would appear just as quickly, and then the PET scan revealed he was in stage three.

I decided to seek advice with the Staff pharmacist Ken at the hospital where I worked. He suggested I speak to a pharmacist that specializes in the area of oncology; he then gave me his sons' name and phone number. For my husband, I would make this phone call as awkward as it could have been, and then the Pharmacist mentioned his son John would be out of town for a week as his new fiancés mother was very ill in another state and they were going to visit her. Oddly enough I had a friend from nursing school, Toni that worked in Hospice that had just gotten engaged, and she was leaving for the same state as her mother was ill.

Again by the Grace of God, that was my friend and her fiancé that specialized in oncology medicine. This was more than a Blessing to my husband it was confirmation of our Heavenly Fathers grace, love and compassion that will sustain us through whatever mountain, big or small, that is in front of us. "I tell you the truth, if anyone says to this mountain, 'Go throw yourself into the sea, and do not doubt in their heart and believe that what he says will happen, it will be done for him. Therefore I tell you, whatever you ask for in prayer, believe that you have received it, and it will be yours." Mark 11:23-24.

The treatments were long and difficult using two other chemo drugs plus the new one. My friends' fiancé had told us if the lymph nodes begin to reduce right away and respond to the treatment that was a good sign. His lymph nodes did respond positively and began to shrink in size bringing much relief to my husband's discomfort.

Working close to home was critical for me still not understanding the depth and breadth of my journey. Never, would my husband and I have ever known how therapeutic and restorative that front porch would be following his chemotherapy treatments. My mother ensured he had a comfortable rocking chair to relax in while enjoying the peacefulness and healing that can only come from Jesus the Great Physician.

Sitting on the front porch with God and His panoramic display of sunsets, constellations, shooting stars and the moon are breathtaking. Our view of the western horizon allows us to experience the marching out of the seasons witnessed by the rising and setting of the sun and moon. "There is a time for everything, and a season for every activity under heaven." Ecclesiastes 3:1.

Out of the Storm comes Noah

During this time, our son decided to join 4H ("About 4-H," 2016). His 4H project to be presented at the local county fair was to raise and train his first puppy. He researched many breeds and became particularly fond of the smaller dogs. The time had arrived for us to pick up his puppy from the breeder; it was almost Spring, being the perfect time to train a puppy.

Getting into the truck I remember him tightly holding onto the piece of colored ribbon the breeder had given him several weeks ago. She had different colored spools of ribbons, as each customer would select a color they liked. After choosing your puppy from the litter, she would cut a large piece of the colored ribbon and gently tie that ribbon around the puppy's neck snipping off a piece for you to bring back when your puppy was ready to be released.

Heading home with the new puppy, we were still about one hour away when it started to get dark, windy and began to rain. As we were driving, my husband called and told us that a tornado was spotted in the vicinity that we were traveling. We were not able to pull off anywhere so we continued driving and getting updates from my husband. As a diversion for both of us, I asked my son what he wanted to name his puppy. After much conversation and distraction in regard to the ongoing storm, he suggested we call him Noah, we all agreed that was a great name.

That summer, his training skills and puppy won my son first prize at the local county fair. I also appreciate that *dog* spelled backward is *God*, being man's best friend, capable of giving unconditional love. That little Noah brought so much love not only to my son; he also became a therapy dog to my husband following his chemo treatments and not feeling so well. Noah instinctively would curl up on his chest providing warmth, comfort, affection and love.

"Anyone who does not love does not know God, because God is love." 1 John 4:8

Brotherly & Sisterly Love

To the north of us, there was a piece of property that became available through a new builder. Since my husband is very close to his brother, he and his wife Belinda decided to purchase that lot and build their new home. I always thought it was kind of amusing, how these two brothers ended up marrying women from New York.

It was fun watching the construction of their new home and the excitement it brings when looking forward to a new journey knowing that family is just 6 acres away. At that time we did not fully understand the Blessing God had for all of us that summer.

Once the new home construction was completed and their house was sold, the fun began packing up boxes and getting ready for the big move out to the country. I am not sure at what point Belinda felt the lump underneath her breast while she was moving boxes, because after that everything became surreal.

John and Belinda now began working together; to find the best cancer treatment team and then their journey as husband and wife for battling cancer began. As a family we supported and loved each as we became prayer warriors and comforters. Again by the grace of God, our beautiful sister Belinda was healed and recovery in her new country home took precedence.

May 1st, 2005 at my sons Confirmation and purposefully choosing the Apostle name John, his certificate proudly reads: Christopher Howard John. Under the circumstances our son was granted permission allowing both his Uncle John and Aunt Belinda to be his sponsors. I will never forget watching the three of them standing together as Bishop Amos completed this sacrament, of being sealed with the gift of the Holy Spirit, and the gust of wind that blew thru the church and rattled all of the open windows.

"They were all together in one place. Suddenly a sound like the blowing of a violent wind came from heaven and filled the whole house where they were sitting. All of them were filled with the Holy Spirit" Acts 2: 1-2 & 4

God Puts Me Where He Needs Me to do His Will & Then He Moves Me...

That summer I took few "as needed" (PRN) positions to be close to home. I met a nursing friend at Jury Duty who offered me a PRN Clinical Coordinator position at her nursing home and also answering an AD to a little community hospital less than 10 miles from our home.

The nursing home is where I met Thomas. Thomas was an older adult that did not socialize much and was often spotted sitting in his room looking out the window or peering out into the hallway. Walking down the hallway, I always wave and said hello to everyone I meet. One day, he called me into his room and said to me "I know you are a Christian and I need to be one." I remember smiling and asking him, how he knew? His simple reply was that he just knew! So I began to ask him some questions about his religion, place of worship and was he receiving any sacraments? He said yes his family was very involved in meeting all of his religious needs, just not his spiritual. He said he could no longer read and did not want to listen to any tapes. I suggested he use a radio and headphones. I explained to him that on the radio there is quite a variety of religious programs available, 24 hours a day, 7 days a week, with more than enough speakers, preachers, authors, artists, and music. He said that was good to know and he thanked me.

The next time I worked at the facility and was passing Thomas' room, I saw him sitting up in a chair with headphones on attached to a radio. I remember smiling at him as the headphones were almost bigger than he was; he excitedly waved me into his room.

He explained how he came to Christ and wanted to recite the prayer of salvation he learned. It was amazing how his family and church came together and gently guided his steps and rekindled the love that he had in his heart for Jesus. What a difference Grace makes!

"And I will put my Spirit in you and move you to follow my decrees and be careful to keep my laws." Ezekiel 36:27.

A Truck Drivers Fare Back to His Rig

The little community hospital ~10 miles from our house was small and quaint. Its setting is rich in history, largely agricultural and surrounded by several Amish communities. Today, that hospital has grown, with a helipad- right alongside the horse and buggy barn.

Approximately 10 miles from the hospital is a very large and busy truck stop. Due to the proximity of the two it is not uncommon for a truck driver to be transported and admitted to the hospital. The oddity is that sometimes there is a local family owned and operated cab service available in the community, and other times, they are just closed for the day.

One particular evening a truck driver was admitted to the hospital for observation. I was scheduled to work the next day, in morning report the nightshift nurse stated the driver would probably be released today since all of his lab work and vital signs were stable.

After completing my assessment, the doctor came in to do rounds and it was determined that the truck driver was to be released today. In reviewing his discharge instructions, the only question he had was the phone number to call the local cab company to take him back to his truck. Unfortunately that was one of the days they were closed. He then called the truck stop to inquire if anyone there was available to pick him up, they told him no.

It was lunch time and a local pastor, I like to call "Padre" came to the hospital to pass out lunch trays and pray or talk with the patients. I told him about the stranded truck driver, so Padre agreed to visit him first. Shortly after, he came out of the patients room smiling. The truck driver insisted on buying all the church raffle tickets Padre had brought to the hospital that day, in lieu of paying anyone else to take him back to his rig at the truck stop.

"And we know that in all things God works for the good of those who love him, who have been called according to His purpose." Romans 8:28

Love and Friendship- Forever

My best friends, through thick & thin are Val & her husband John, who has also experienced some challenging, serious health issues. A few years ago, Val called me on the phone deeply concerned, explaining that her husband was critically ill and has been admitted to their local community hospital, Intensive Care Unit (ICU). He had been given multiple blood transfusions more than the average patient receives, albeit until the doctors could locate the internal bleed it was futile. The last call from Val was that the medical team was going to insert a central line and transport him to the main campus. I agreed; as there is more talent and resources downtown that he would benefit from. I also let her know I was on my way.

As I arrived on the floor, I saw Val and her daughter and we talked briefly. I then went to see John before they transported him. Heading toward his room, I saw three medical staff entering, so I followed them. Standing at the bedside was the intervention team explaining the procedure, the need for consent, and the urgency of inserting the central line. Looking up they asked who I was. I told them I was part of the team; John looked at me, shook his head and smiled.

Lightheartedly, I then said I was his girlfriend wanting to see him before he was transferred. This "girlfriend line" has been going on for years. In tough medical situations it alleviates some of the stress, anxiety and makes him smile. With his permission, I looked at his vital signs and lab work. I was happy to learn he was somewhat stable. Thanks be to God.

Once Val, her daughter and I arrived at the main campus, we went to the unit where he was being admitted. The medical team, along with the Doctor, had completed their admission paperwork and assured all of us of the benefits of being admitted to this teaching hospital, and more importantly, how he would be carefully monitored and kept safe throughout the night.

"A man of many companions may come to ruin, but there is a friend who sticks closer than a brother." Proverbs 18:24

Melting the ICE

I am still an avid hockey fan, just like my mother, who took me to my first NHL game in Buffalo New York. When I was a kid I played field hockey, street hockey and ice hockey. When my son started to play, I noticed an invitation for women to play ice hockey on a summer league. After purchasing the entire garb, which one must now wear for safety, it took quite awhile to learn how to just move with all of that stuff on, let alone skate.

The second summer I played, I had a patient on our unit in the hospital who was waiting for a heart transplant. The common thread for us became hockey. He shared with me that he was friends with one of the coaches from the Buffalo Sabres "back in the day." I told him I had season tickets for the Sabres "back in the day." I also told him about our women's ice hockey team and how excited I was to be on the ice again, he then asked me to take a team picture.

As time went on, and he stayed on the recipient list for a heart, I felt the Holy Spirit telling me that I must talk to him about his language and using the Lords name in vain. Wow, this was not going to be easy. Finally one day, I sat down to talk to him and the words just came out of my mouth, "I don't think I would damn or curse God, as you might be seeing him sooner than you think." He told me he was glad I started that conversation, as he has been thinking a lot lately about his life, where he has been.... and where he will be going.

He agreed to a visit from pastoral care and the next time I saw him, he told me he had given his life to Jesus. I was his nurse one more time, as they were getting ready to transfer him as a donor heart became available. We said good bye and he thanked me for bringing back some great hockey memories along with taking the picture of our women's ice hockey team. I was not sure where he went for his new heart, but one thing I do know for sure is where he will be spending eternity.

"I will give you a new heart and put a new spirit in you; I will remove from you your heart of stone and give you a heart of flesh. And I will put my spirit in you and move you to follow my decrees and be careful to keep my laws."Ezekiel 36:26-28.

On Gods Team Now

In the hospital hallways are little nurses' stations that have heightened chairs to sit on for charting or looking up data on the computer. One morning a physician came alongside and pushed me off the chair, not saying a word. As much as I was shocked, I also became speechless, or God had gently placed his hand over my mouth.

I went to the cafeteria at lunchtime and ran into one of the nurses on my hockey team. I needed to talk to someone so I told her what happened. I felt much better after we spoke and had eaten lunch and was now re-charged and ready to go back to the floor.

Later in the afternoon, that same Physician came to the unit and apologized to me. He also asked if there was anything he could do to make it up to me. Jokingly I said yea; "meet me on the ice some day." His response was very odd and almost shaky, saying he had just heard that I played hockey and how much I loved the sport. We talked for quite some time and again he apologized and wanted to make sure our relationship was okay. I assured him we were fine.

Just before my shift was over; the friend that I had lunch with came up to my unit to speak to me. She had asked if the physician that I spoke to her about came up to the floor and apologized. I told her yes. She started to smile, as she has been a nurse at this hospital for quite a few years and was very familiar with most of the physicians. She began to tell me how she enlightened that doctor as to what degree of a hockey fanatic I truly was. She then explained that I played defense and was a very aggressive player. Finally, she laughed and said, "I also told him you keep all your gear and sticks in your truck." At that point he said, "I probably need to go and apologize."

"Do not repay anyone for evil for evil. Be careful to do what is right in the eyes of everybody. If it is possible, as far as it depends on you, live in peace with everyone."Romans 12:17-18". "So then, each of us will give an account of himself to God." Romans 14:12."

Granny Adoption

One morning after assessing my patients, I spoke to one of my female patients about signing her consent form for a colonoscopy, as we needed to start the prep. She told me she was refusing to sign the consent and refusing to have that procedure. Understanding Patients Rights, I said okay knowing I would speak to her again. As I was walking out, the roommate in bed one whispered to me to come forward. She said to me, "you need to talk and listen to her story." She informed me that her roommate was up all night crying and explaining how she had fallen at home and that one of the medical responders and his wife are in the process of adopting her as their "Grandmother."

After completing my morning documentation, I went and spoke to the older female adult in bed two. She began to tell me some of the detailed behavior of the medical responder and his wife, stating how they made her eat a full jar of beets and that is why her stool is red. She told me her husband had passed away and that she lived alone on a 100 plus acres of prime property that builders want to purchase and develop. She was completely alert and oriented to person, place and time. She expressed to me that the adoption date is coming up and that is why the couple wanted her in the hospital. During this conversation a young man came into the room to ensure she would be going for that colonoscopy today. My patient became visibly shaken and fearful, I asked this visitor to step outside the room. In the hallway, he grabbed the consent paper out of my hand and said, "She will be having this procedure today, I can get her to sign it." Following him into her room and asking who he was, he refused to answer. At that point, I demanded he give me the consent form and asked him to leave the room or I would call security.

Immediately, I went to the phone and paged the patients' physician. When the doctor returned my call, I explained everything that had happened this morning, especially the threatening manner in which this supposed "grandson to be" was demonstrating. I also gave an account of some of the unpleasant stories this woman had shared with me as she tearfully admitted being afraid of this couple. She could not understand how she could just be adopted as someone's Grandmother. The physician then asked if we were talking about the same person, stating that every time the emergency medical person and his wife brought that patient/woman into her office she could barely walk, talk, or answer even the simplest questions.

Upon arrival to the floor, the Doctor immediately went into this woman's room and spent several hours with her. After a thorough assessment the Doctor asked if I could meet with her. I gave report on my patients, telling the charge nurse I would be off the unit for lunch.

The physician admitted this is the first time she had seen this patient alert and oriented.
She indeed was able to answer every question clearly and succinctly. The patient was also able to share some of the details and events that were occurring in her life related to this couple. It was agreed upon that no more tests or procedures were to be performed and that the Judge in this adoption case would be notified immediately.

Protective Services placed a notice on the patients door reading "All visitors must report to the nurses' station before entering," as they were now involved.

The physician contacted me later to inform me that the Judge was instrumental in finding a trustworthy legal guardian to oversee this woman's personal matters and to keep her safe.

At the end of my shift I thanked the patient in bed one for trusting me, and the patient in bed two thanked me for taking the time to listen to her story and believe.

"Religion that God our Father accepts as pure and faultless is this: to look after the orphans and widows in their own distress and to keep oneself from being polluted by the world." James 1:27.

Look, Listen & Feel His Love

Often times I would pick up shifts in the ambulatory recovery room. This is where patients would have an outpatient procedure such as a cardiac catherization, or a special procedure that did not require a hospital stay. I enjoyed working in this setting; it was a small glimpse of the surgery world, a change in nursing style with a diverse flavor of personalities.

In my career, I have received a variety of accolades. One of my favorites was delivered to me several weeks after I had taken care of a female patient in the recovery room. She told me that when she rides her bicycle and listens to her radio, she hears the most beautiful love songs from God to her and she was not referring to Christian music.

I then shared one of my favorite experiences. At a certain time of the day, the shadow from the sun reflects the utility poles onto the country road in the shape of a cross. I explained that every time I ride over that shadow of the cross with my silhouette, I am reminded how Jesus died on the cross for such a sinner like me.

A few weeks later in my mailbox at work, there was an overstuffed, legal size envelope that read "for the nurse who rides a bike." I smiled when I began to open this, as I knew exactly who it was from.

The title she penned on the first page read; How the Creator speaks to Humanity in Songs. The following pages contained hand written song titles dating from the late 70s, 80s and 90s. In total, there were 90 of her favorite song titles that she synchronized with Bible verses from both the Old and New Testament to the chorus. The common theme throughout her testimony was the unfathomable love our Heavenly Father has for all of His children and how He shares His beauty around the world in everything He has creates and displays.

"How great is the love the Father has lavished on us, that we should be called children of God." John 3:1.

The Friendship Walk

My family was made up of four children. I was the youngest of the girls and my brother was four years younger than me. We went to Christian schools as my parents were devout Catholics. My Father was quite the disciplinarian, demanding honor and respect along with teaching us to live according to the 10 Commandments.

By no means was I a girly girl. Whatever the sport for that season was: I was on a team playing it. The Alabama Swamps in New York, was a great place for trailblazing through the marshes and swamps as I would arrive at home with a completely mud covered truck. Oh, my dad would just shake his head and tell me to get that dirty/muddy truck off of his driveway!

It was not until after I had my son, did I ever really understand my father. As parents, we want or even expect our kids to be perfect. I found out later, how embarrassed my father was telling the neighbors, that was his daughters' truck in the driveway and not his sons.

When my Father became very ill and my mother was unable to care for him, he was placed in a nursing home. I had been a nurse for awhile, so our time and visits together became more and more precious. I would comb and wash his hair, face, hands and trim him up to be the handsome man he was. I would then take him outside in his wheelchair. I pushed him along a walking path that was called the "Friendship Walk" and yes indeed, how appropriate and significant that became.

I knew my Father enjoyed watching cars, so one day we sat by the roadside under a large tree, enjoying the fall weather and sunshine. Suddenly, I heard him say "hey," looking over at me, and then saying it again. He was never very talkative; he was a quiet, conservative man, always telling me I was his loquacious daughter. Then I said "hey" after feeling something hit the top of my head. The squirrels were in the tree above us collecting acorns and occasionally dropping one or two. I showed him what was landing on our heads, and with the most loving look in his eyes, he gently smiled at me.

"Train a child in the way they should go, and when they are old they will not turn from it." Proverbs 22:6

Memory Lane

One Friday during the summer, I told my friends I was on my way to New York to go window shopping with my Mother. Explaining replacement windows, that she could open, close and clean. After comparing and pricing, we placed the order with a delivery date of the first two weeks of September, thankfully I had requested vacation time for sons my Birthday those weeks.

Winter was now upon us, as it was February and my mother's caregiver went to visit her a day early, thank goodness as she found my mother very ill; she was transported and hospitalized with Pneumonia. At the time of discharge the Doctor strongly suggested she be placed in Assisted Living (AL); my brother thoughtfully located a facility between her two best friends from High School, Ginny and Betty my Godmother.

A few years later she suffered a stroke. Unfortunately her level of care had drastically changed and she was no longer appropriate for AL; therefore my brother thoughtfully moved her closer to family members.

Two weeks before Mothers day 2015 I went to visit her. Upon arrival she was somewhat hesitant to leave, the staff and I encouraged her that going out for a ride would be good. Our trip this time included driving around Goat Island in Niagara Falls, visiting her parents Chapel in Pendleton, New York and stopping at her favorite little country store and then to lunch.

While in the store something strange happened. The clerk asked my mother who she was with. Sadly my mother got embarrassed maybe even a little frustrated as she could not verbalize my name. I had noticed her frequently looking over at me in the car and now realizing the effects of the stroke and the difficulty she was having with her speech.

Leaving the store and in the car, I started to tear up; as she sat there looking out the car window. I wish I could have taken her back to Ohio like we used to, and sit in the Adirondack chairs by the campfire, watching the shooting stars until 1 or 2 in morning, talking and laughing and reminiscing about the past, while enjoying the present. One thing I loved about my mother was how she faithfully prayed every morning for her children and anyone else on her prayer list. What a prayer warrior she was just like her mother Martha.

"Honor your Father and your Mother, so that you may live long in the land the Lord your God is giving you." Exodus 20:12

Living for the Lord

A few years after both of my parents had passed from this life, we received some unexpected money. My husband and I agreed to spend this on a necessity, something we *need* but would not want to spend money on. Since we only have one child, we agreed to purchase our cemetery site and have everything in order. In meeting with our parish Sexton, there was one site available behind the chapel by a tree, how appropriate we remarked and proceeded forward.

One morning I decided to ride my bicycle to our parish in the Valley. This would be twice the distance, therefore I had decided ahead of time to stop at the Chapel for prayer and rest.

The beauty of our Chapel, dated 1861, with its chestnut wood altars, spectacular stained glass windows, pipe organ, and beckoning 90 foot steeple, reminds us of God's ever presence in our lives, and our due diligence to be reverent.

Leaving the chapel, I walked back to the cemetery and sat on a bench facing the 20 foot tall, white axed, granite cross (St. Martin of Tours, n.d., 1996) meditating and praying. I walked my bike over to our gravesite, as the caretaker called over and asking if I would like the grass trimmed. I smiled; telling him it looked just fine and then thanked him.

Taking my right foot I tamped down the overgrown grass and then lightly tapped the inscription "Nurse Nicholette." Truly believing that heaven is just on the other side, smiling to my Heavenly Father I thought, "Thank goodness I know where I am going, as I have confirmed my reservation in the non-smoking section of eternity."(N.Tixier/personal quote, 2010).

Hopping on my bike and returning to the road a hearse went by and then one funeral car after another. Looking up at the sky and smiling at Gods sense of humor, I saw the most beautiful cloud in the shape of a cross.

Mother and Child

Before my bike ride, I check the temperature, wind velocity and direction, as it is easier to ride into the wind heading out and allow the wind to assist in returning me home. One morning according to the wind I took a right turn out of out our driveway, heading north.

Passing a young mother jogging with her daughter in a stroller, the wobbly plastic wheels trying to keep pace in the stony road, reminded me of the days I ran competitively with my son in a baby jogger. I would register both of our names. Since he crossed the finish line first, he would always beat my time.

I decided to turn around and talk to that young mother. Riding alongside, I told her about the baby jogger hanging in our garage and asked her if she would like to have it?

Smiling and looking at me she said, "You don't recognize me?" I stepped off my bike to walk with her only to find out; she was one of my son's best friends from high school. It had been about 8 years since I attended her graduation party and what a beautiful young woman and mother she has become.

Haleah is always welcome at our home. One of my fondest memories of her was the wonderful handmade chocolate covered strawberries she made for me one Mother's Day. Walking up our driveway, she told my husband and I that this was a turnaround for her morning jog, as she would rest and check on her beautiful little girl.

My husband retrieved the baby jogger dangling from the rafters and proceeded to fill the tires, then stating he wanted to check out everything and clean it up. We told her we would bring it over later. I couldn't wait to tell my son about the jogger and who we gave it to. As a family, we are glad it is being used, and even happier that we love the person who will be using it.

"Love the Lord your God with all your heart and with all your soul and with all your mind. This is the first and greatest commandment. And the second is like it: Love your neighbor as yourself." Matthew 22: 37-39.

The Hardest Job I Will Ever Love

I love the autonomy nursing has to offer. Excitedly, I took my first position as an Administrative Nursing Supervisor on night shift at a hospital in the inner city. This facility had 200+ beds and very busy medical and psychiatric emergency rooms. In my career, this is where I came up with the phrase, "You know when there is 10 minutes left in the football game and it goes on for another hour? Well let me tell you about Nursing Supervisor time." (N.Tixier/personal quote, 2007).

At this hospital, it was not unusual to have a forensic (under arrest) patient admitted to one of the units accompanied by a police officer. As the house supervisor it was our duty and responsibility to monitor these rooms. One week I became very familiar with a certain male patient that kept requesting to speak to the night shift supervisor.

During one visit this patient began to cry and become extremely emotional and remorseful. He asked if I could find him a Bible. Upon my return to his room with the Good Book, he hurriedly looked up a passage and asked the police officer if he would be allowed to kneel on the floor and asking if I would join him. As his request was granted, in a childlike manner, he gently knelt at the side of the hospital bed, still hand cuffed to the bedrail, weeping and reading Acts 3:19 "repent, then, and turn to God, so that your sins may be wiped out, that times of refreshing may come from the Lord, and that He may send the Christ, who has been appointed for you- even Jesus."

I don't remember how long we knelt on that floor; I do recall how surreal this experience became. It was as if that entire room was transformed to the most beautiful, peaceful place on earth as it filled with the light and love of Jesus. No one said a word or moved, the officers' radio never chirped, my pager never beeped, no call light rang, no noise in the hallway, just a peace beyond all understanding filled that room and our hearts that night. 'There is rejoicing in the presence of the angels of God over one sinner who repents." Luke 15:10.

Choirs of Angles

I have come to appreciate working in a hospital that is built around a Chapel. Night shift is very challenging, therefore seeking wisdom and guidance before my shift became routine.

One evening due to heavy traffic, I went to the nursing office first, got report, and then went to the Chapel to pray. It was a couple of days before Christmas and the church was decorated beautifully. The smell of fresh pine from the Christmas trimmings around the Nativity scene and the live wreaths hanging on the pillars filled the church with the aroma of Christmas.

As I knelt down and closed my eyes to pray, I recalled a part of my orientation a little over a month ago, that included a Blessing of the hands in this chapel. The ceremony was beautiful, although, more importantly was the confirmation from God that I was here for His purpose and plan.

During this reflection the most beautiful instrumental Christmas music began to play, sounding like a choir of angels as the heavenly hosts filled the little Chapel. As much as I would have enjoyed sitting there for awhile praying and basking in the heavenly sounds of Christmas, I needed to start my rounds for the night.

Walking down the hall that connects the Chapel to the hospital, strategically placed is the Protective Services Command Center. Every shift I always stop to say hello. This particular night I told the Officer how I enjoyed the beautiful Christmas music in the Chapel. Taking his eyes away from the monitors and looking at me, he said, "Unless there were musicians on the altar, or a live choir up in the loft that is impossible, as there has not been a sound system or speakers in that Chapel for years." Then smiling at me he said, "you're not the first person to report that to me this week and you won't be the last, and by the way, Merry Christmas."

"The Lord your God is with you, He is mighty to save. He will take great delight in you, He will quiet you with His love, He will rejoice over you with singing." Zephaniah 3:17

The Spirit of Giving is Contagious

The Church we first attended when we moved to the country was very involved in community outreach to much of the rural/agricultural community. One program they promoted was to anonymously adopt a child until they turned 18 years old and provide them with a yearly Birthday and Christmas gift.

This Blessing transformed us from the hustle and bustle of family gift giving to the pure joy of giving to others; agreeing to choose a boy that was the same age as our son.

As a family we looked forward to his wish list, which at times, was as humble as requesting underwear, socks and slippers. My son would also think of something popular at the time for "his age" and add that gift to the package that would be delivered to the church.

One Christmas we went to my parents in New York for a couple of days. Since my son was older, they gave him money as they did with their other grandchildren. He was into skateboards at the time, and there was a shop in the mall close to my parents' home where he went to customize and build his own skateboard, choosing all the pieces and parts for his design.

Arriving back in Ohio and Christmas break coming to an end, he wanted to show his uniquely designed skateboard from New York to his friends, so he took it to school.

At school my son asked all of his friends if they had a good Christmas and one of his friends stated it was not a good year for him and his father. When lunch was over, my son went to his locker, took out his new skateboard and placed it into that friend's locker.

In the years to follow, we expanded our outreach of goodwill by volunteering locally, and globally partnering with organizations that provide food and farm animals around the world.

"In everything I did, I showed you that by this kind of hard work we must help the weak, remembering the words the Lord Jesus himself said: "It is more blessed to give than to receive."Acts 20:35.

34

Nick at Night

As I became more comfortable in my new hospital environment and Administrative role, I greatly appreciated the welcoming I received, understanding that sometimes it is very difficult being the new person. Most significant was the respectful relationships made with the Doctors, Residents, Nurses, Therapists, Protective Services, Maintenance, and the Hospital Operator.

One night during my rounds, a nurse referred to me as "nick @ night," smiling and thinking to myself that is a very gracious nickname. I immediately began to recall how Nicodemus, a Pharisee, chose to travel at night to visit Jesus. There are many theories and thoughts in regard to why he chose that time to travel. Agreeably, most people do work during the day, which may be one of the reasons he went at night. Conceivably, was it cooler with fewer people to contend with on the road? Or, was he afraid people would see where he was going, and to whom he was going to visit?

Looking back, I visited Jesus countless times throughout my nightshift. I would take distraught, sorrowful, and bereaved, visitors, siblings, parents, grandparents, friends, employees and even patients to the chapel at night. As many times in my position, I was totally incapable of being able to console or comfort many of the sorrows and pain that can be anywhere, and in any hospital. The only comfort I could offer was to take them to their Heavenly Fathers house and sit quietly as they cried or lamented to Jesus, their Lord and Savior. One of the nurses on nightshift asked how I kept my faith and disposition intact. I told her "God is my Primary Care Physician, Jesus is my cardiologist and the Holy Spirit is my Counselor."(N. Tixier, Spring, 2007)

"Come to me, all you who are weary and burdened, and I will give you rest. Take my yoke upon you and learn from me, for I am gentle and humble in heart, and you will find rest for your souls. For my yoke is easy and my burden is light." Matthew 11:28.

It's not what it looks like.

Code Brown in an Ohio hospital is a missing adult patient. Hospitals may refine the code and give a description of the patient along with a person that may be accompanying them.

One day, I agreed to work dayshift, 7am-7pm for co-worker. At about 6:30pm, almost the end of my shift a code Brown was called. The overhead page at first was indistinguishable, not giving too much information in regard to the patient/description. Therefore grabbing a two-way radio form the nursing office to communicate with protective services, off I went.

The operator finally paged out a little more information and description, as vague as it was, it could have been a number of female patients, walking around in a hospital gown pushing an IV pole, escorted by a male. The second page came over with a little more detail as to the color of her hair, height and weight and the description of the gentleman she was with. It was then disclosed over the two-way radio that a nurse overheard the patient stating she wanted to go outside to smoke a cigarette.

A staff member from a higher floor saw a female patient with an IV pole and a male companion, down by the bus shelter smoking a cigarette. This newfound discovery was announced over the two-way radios, therefore changing directions, I headed toward the front of the hospital.

Upon arriving at the front doors of the hospital, I ran out of the hospital flying down the first set of steps and the long pathway before another flight of steps and finally arriving at the bus stop. Thank goodness Protective Services was right behind me, as this patient stated they were not feeling very well, telling us she felt like passing out. Therefore one of the officers ran back to the hospital to get a gurney instead of the wheelchair.

Safe inside the hospital and up to the surgical floor we returned the patient, although the rumors had already begun. The 7pm employees arriving in their cars and waiting to swipe into the parking garage and watching this unfold, surmised that I must have done something really bad, to be running the way I was, and Protective Services chasing me the way they were. "So we fix our eyes not on what is seen, but on what is unseen. For what is seen is temporary, but what is unseen is eternal." 2 Corinthians 4:18

What is that in the Ditch?

In the cooler fall season, I wait for the temperature to reach between 40-50 degrees before heading out on my bicycle. One particular afternoon it took until 2:00 pm to get to that range.

On the last leg of my ride, I noticed some colored flags ahead and something in the ditch. Finally arriving at the scene, there was a recumbent bicycle with an older male sitting in the ditch. Introducing myself I attempted to help him out, although he was too weak, and the ditch was too steep.

After several attempts a delivery truck came along so I flagged it down. Working together, the driver of the truck stated, "I passed this person quite some time ago and now regret that I did not stop earlier to help." Once we assisted the gentleman and his recumbent bicycle back on the road, I asked him where he was headed. He told me he parked his car by the church where the town square is, I agreed to escort him back.

Once we were arrived in the middle of the town, we found his car & trailer parked by the church. I went over to the mechanic shop and asked the owner if he knew what time that car had pulled into the parking lot? He told me around 9:00 that morning. Now I was concerned, it was past 3:00pm, wondering how long he had been in that ditch, especially with the earlier cooler temperatures.

I started a barrage of questions from a nursing stand point especially how he ended up in the ditch and did he have any injuries? I then extend my hand for a handshake to access his body temperature and was concerned that I might need to notify someone.

I asked him how far he rode today. He told me he went 10 miles west to the next town to meet some friends for lunch. I was familiar with the restaurant he mentioned, and then calculating the time and distance for his journey, I concluded that he and his recumbent bike might not have been in that ditch too very long. He continued to load his bike onto the trailer, refusing any help, telling me he was 84 years young and that since purchasing his recumbent bike in spring he has peddled over 1,000 miles.

"Do nothing out of selfish ambition or vain conceit, but in humility consider others better than yourselves." Philippians 2: 3.

Due Respect to Veterans

There is a day set aside in November in the United States to honor, pray and give thanks to all of our Veterans that served and sacrificed their lives to provide security and safety for you and me.

One Veterans day while working in the hospital I was made aware that we had an older adult Veteran admitted to our Medical/Surgical unit. Over time I have learned from friends and family the long term affect that these men and women are subject to, and whether they have, or have not, been able to prevail over what they have seen, experienced or done.

Knocking on the door and introducing myself I entered this man's room. There were no lights or television on, and the bed next to him was empty. I sat down on a chair by his bedside and started the conversation with gratitude and thankfulness for his service. He remained nonverbal for a couple of minutes and then began to weep so bitterly it brought me to tears. I took his hand as the room became filled with his sorrow and pain and finally he said he needed to tell me something he has never shared with anyone else.

Through his tears, he revealed some of the horrific details he was ordered to do to other humans, known as the enemy. He further stated that he has been plagued his entire life with nightmares. He stated he has never told his wife or children what he had done, fearing the loss of their respect, love or even the possibility they would become afraid of him.

I encouraged him to seek counsel. I then offered to notify our hospital pastoral care which he accepted, explaining that they can provide other resources that are available. I stayed in his room for quite some time that night, letting him talk and then praying together. In the morning at the end of my shift, I went to his room to hug him goodbye.

"Carry each other's burdens, and in this way you will fulfill the law of Christ." Galatians 6:2. "Therefore, as we have opportunity, let us do good to all people, especially to those who belong to the family of believers." Galatians 6:10

Come Holy Spirit and Fill Our Hearts

In Ohio we like to describe our winter months as battleship gray days. It's where the gray sunless skies mesh with the dormant colorless landscape of the earth. We long for the warm spring sunshine that produces the buds of life on the tree and in our gardens.

Down by the tree line in front of our home I have a red painted galvanized garbage can with whimsical painted white letters that read, "For the Birds." Storing birdseed where my birdfeeders are located makes it easier to keep them full, especially when it is bitter cold.

For Christmas one year, my husband bought me a guidebook that provides names and pictures of the variety of birds native to Ohio. Among some of my fine feathered friends are the colored finches, sparrows, chickadees, bluebirds, red headed wood peckers, swallows, red tail hawk, turkey buzzards and the Screech owl that lives in the woods behind our property.

My favorite of all species is the Ohio State Red Cardinal, remembering the first time I saw one. It was during the latter part of winter, perched on one of our barren fruit trees in the backyard. It caught my eye looking out of our kitchen window as it was such a brilliant red in contrast to the gray. At that time I was not sure what it was, so I acknowledged the fact that the Holy Spirit was paying me a visit and making me aware of His ever presence.

Every time thereafter if sitting on the porch, riding in the car, walking, biking, visiting neighbors or talking to the mail carrier, whenever I see a Red Cardinal cross my path, I always smile and love to say, "There goes the Holy Spirit."(N.Tixier/personal quote 2012)

"Come Holy Spirit, fill the hearts of your faithful and enkindle in them the fire of your love. O, God, who by the light of the Holy Spirit, did instruct the hearts of the faithful, grant us in the same Spirit to be truly wise and ever to rejoice in His consolation. Through Christ Our Lord Amen."

Ike's Story

In November 2013 we adopted a Shih Tzu named Ike from a rescue organization. My husband and I learned earlier to appreciate the ease of caring for a smaller breed dog. We drove to Columbus to meet with the foster parents and our possible little adoptee. He was the sweetest little dog and this being their first foster, they requested time alone with him before we departed.

Six months later, in the spring of 2014, around 9:30 pm, the tornado siren sounded in our township. My husband and I quickly donned our socks and shoes, grabbed our communication devices and Ike, and headed into the basement. Adhesively attached under each basement step is a battery operated light. Sitting down on our supply coolers and reaching up, we turned each one on, just as the power went out. We sat on the coolers that contain water, meds, emergency supplies, radio, blankets, and pillows along with a bracket of our son's various sporting helmets.

In moments to follow we received a frantic text from the previous foster parents as they watched the news realizing the tornado was heading right toward our home and Ike.

When the all clear was given, Ike texted his beloved family in Columbus and told them not to worry, as Nicholette and her husband are very active members in the County Medical Reserve Corp. (MRC, 2017) through their county Health Department. He told them not to worry as the set up they have in their basement under their stairs is phenomenal.

I have been an active volunteer in the MRC since 2007. Emergency preparedness has given me a new role in my nursing profession that goes beyond the hospital walls and into the community, understanding the basic need to take care of ourselves so that we can help others.

"I love you, O lord my strength. The Lord is my rock, my fortress and my deliverer; my God is my rock, in whom I take refuge. He is my shield and the horn of my salvation, my stronghold." Psalm 18:1-2.

References

4-H | Positive Youth Development and Mentoring Organization. (2016). Retrieved from http://4-h.org/about/what-is-4-h/

Holy Bible. (1984). Grand Rapids, Michigan: Zondervan.

Medical Reserve Corps. (2012). Retrieved from http://www.medinahealth.org/

Sacred Landmarks (2010). Retrieved from http://www.sacredlandmarks.us/ohio/medina-county/st-martin-of-tours-chapel/

The History of St. Martin of Tours Valley City1822 - 1900 - 2000. (n.d.). Retrieved from http://www.stmartinvc.org/ParishHistory/1900.html

About the Author

Nicholette Tixier MSN,RN is compassionate about helping others, whether she is in the clinical setting teaching nursing students or as a first responder in aiding others. She is an active volunteer in her church and community. Her life-long passion is to continue to inspire and encourage others to engage in acts of servanthood, kindness and goodwill. She advises people to volunteer if they cannot find fulfillment in their jobs. In 2015 after completing her Masters in Nursing Leadership and Management she received the Inaugural Nurse Inspiration Award from the Healthcare organization where she was employed.

In 2014, she received an Honorable Mention award from the American Red Cross "Acts of Courage" in regard to ordinary individuals performing extraordinary acts in times of emergencies.

In 2012 and 2017 she received the Volunteer Of the Year award for service and dedication to the Medina County Medical Reserve Corps.

Printed in the United States
By Bookmasters